I0866511

PLANET

MERCURY

By Emily Kington

CONTENTS

First published in 2026 by Hungry Tomato Ltd
F15, Old Bakery Studios, Blewetts Wharf, Malpas Road,
Truro, Cornwall, TR1 1QH, UK.

Copyright © 2026 Hungry Tomato Ltd

No part of this publication may be reproduced, stored in a retrieval system, or transmitted in any form or by any means, electronic, mechanical, photocopying, recording, or otherwise, without prior written permission of the copyright owner. A CIP catalog record for this book is available from the British Library.

ISBN 9781835696750

Manufactured in the USA

Discover more at
www.hungrytomato.com

Front cover image is an artist's impression of Mercury and the Messenger spacecraft. Mercury is shown in false-colour. Title page image is an edited image of Mercury. Contents page image is an edited image of Mercury.

Words in **BOLD** can be found in the glossary.

WHERE IS MERCURY?

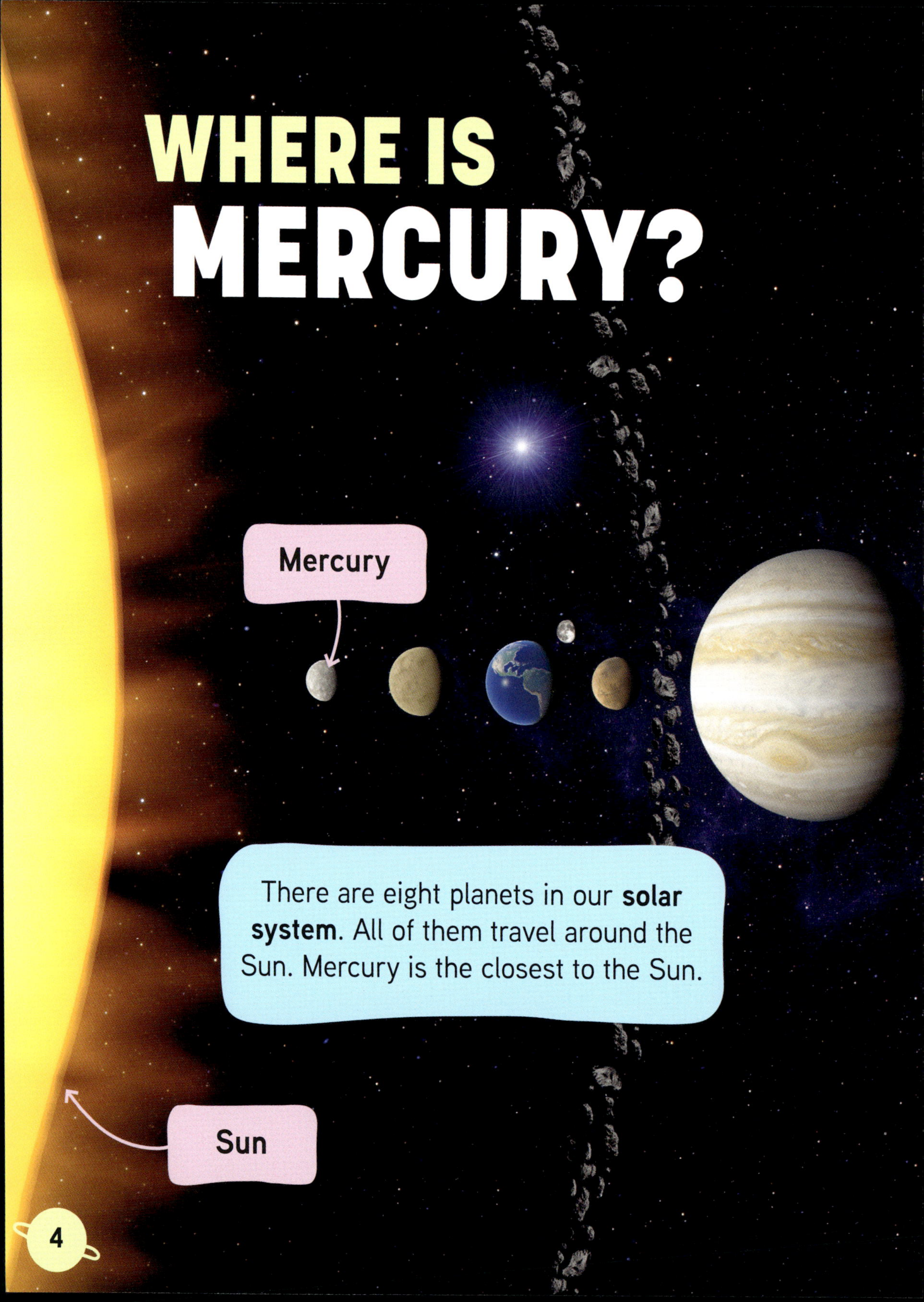

There are eight planets in our **solar system**. All of them travel around the Sun. Mercury is the closest to the Sun.

The time it takes for a planet to travel around the Sun once is called a year. Mercury travels around the Sun once every 88 **Earth days**. This journey is called its **orbit**.

Mercury's orbit around the Sun is shaped like an egg!

PLANET FACTS

Planets are always spinning. A day is the time it takes a planet to spin around once.

One day on Mercury lasts for 176 Earth days. A year on Mercury is 88 Earth days, making a day on Mercury twice as long as a year!

Mercury orbits the Sun faster than any other planet in our solar system at 104,400 miles per hour (169,200 kilometers per hour)!

WHY IS MERCURY SO HEAVY?

Mercury is a rocky planet. It is also the smallest planet in the solar system.

If Mercury were the size of a golf ball, Earth would be the size of a grapefruit!

Even though it is the smallest planet, Mercury is heavy for its size. Scientists think its iron-rich **core** makes up most of the planet's total size.

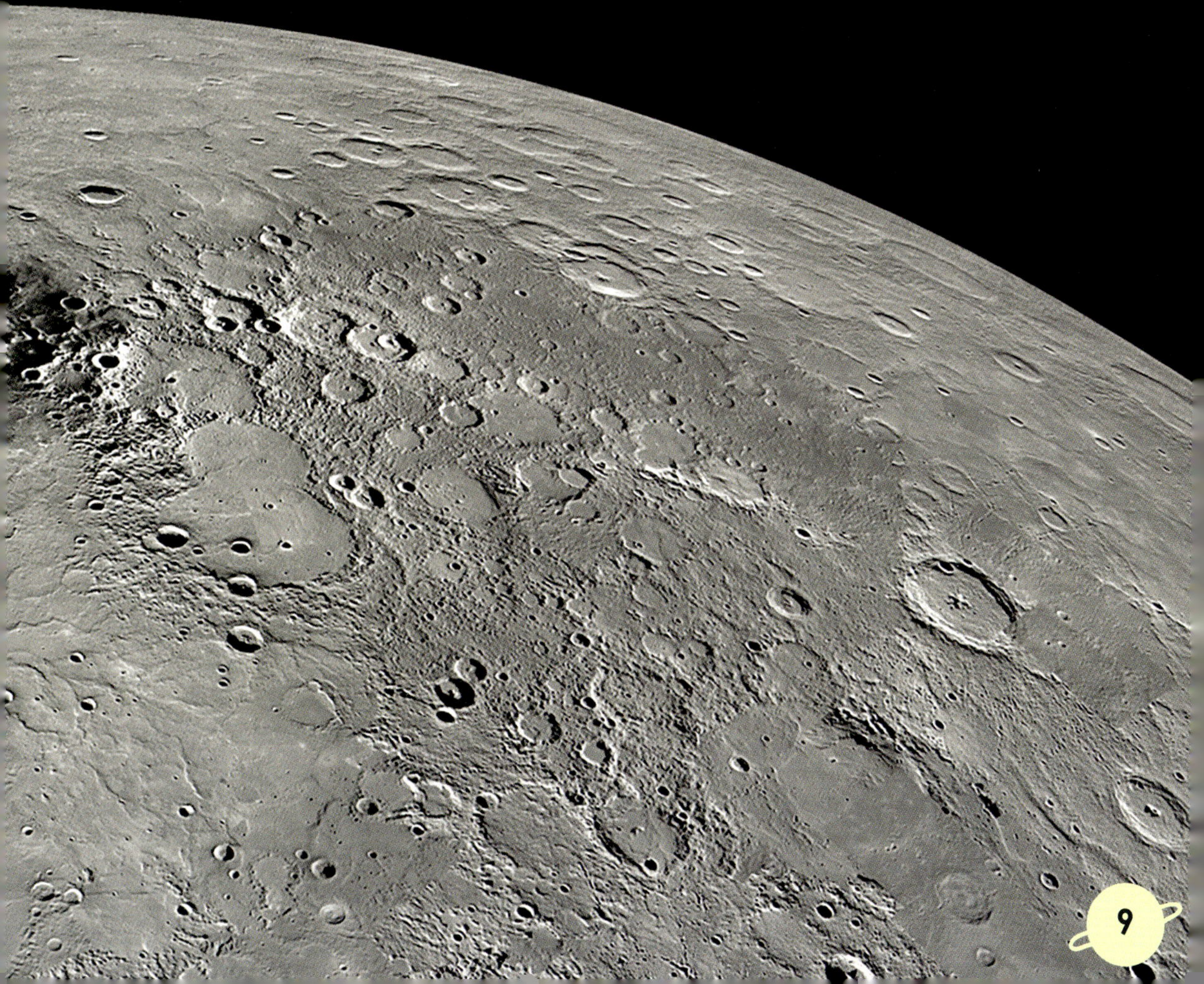

COULD WE LIVE ON MERCURY?

Living on Mercury would be very difficult. There is no air to breathe, and it gets very hot during the day on the side of the planet that faces the Sun.

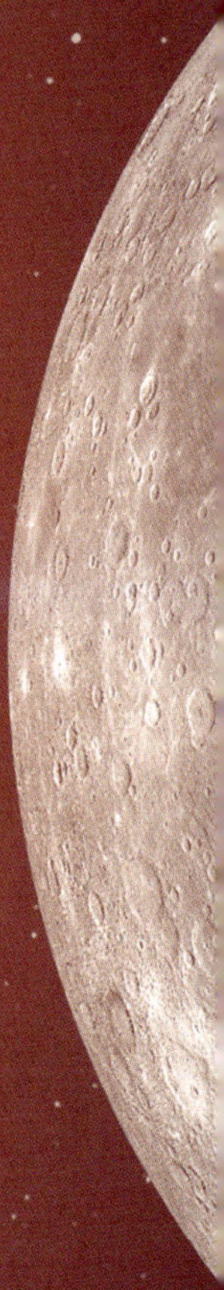

Earth's **atmosphere** holds in heat like a blanket. But on Mercury there is no atmosphere, so it gets extremely cold on the side that doesn't face the Sun.

Mercury is also hit with a lot of **solar radiation** that is very harmful to humans and machines.

AN AMAZING DISCOVERY

Mercury is one of the most difficult planets to study because of where it is – right next to the Sun! Only three missions have ever been sent toward Mercury.

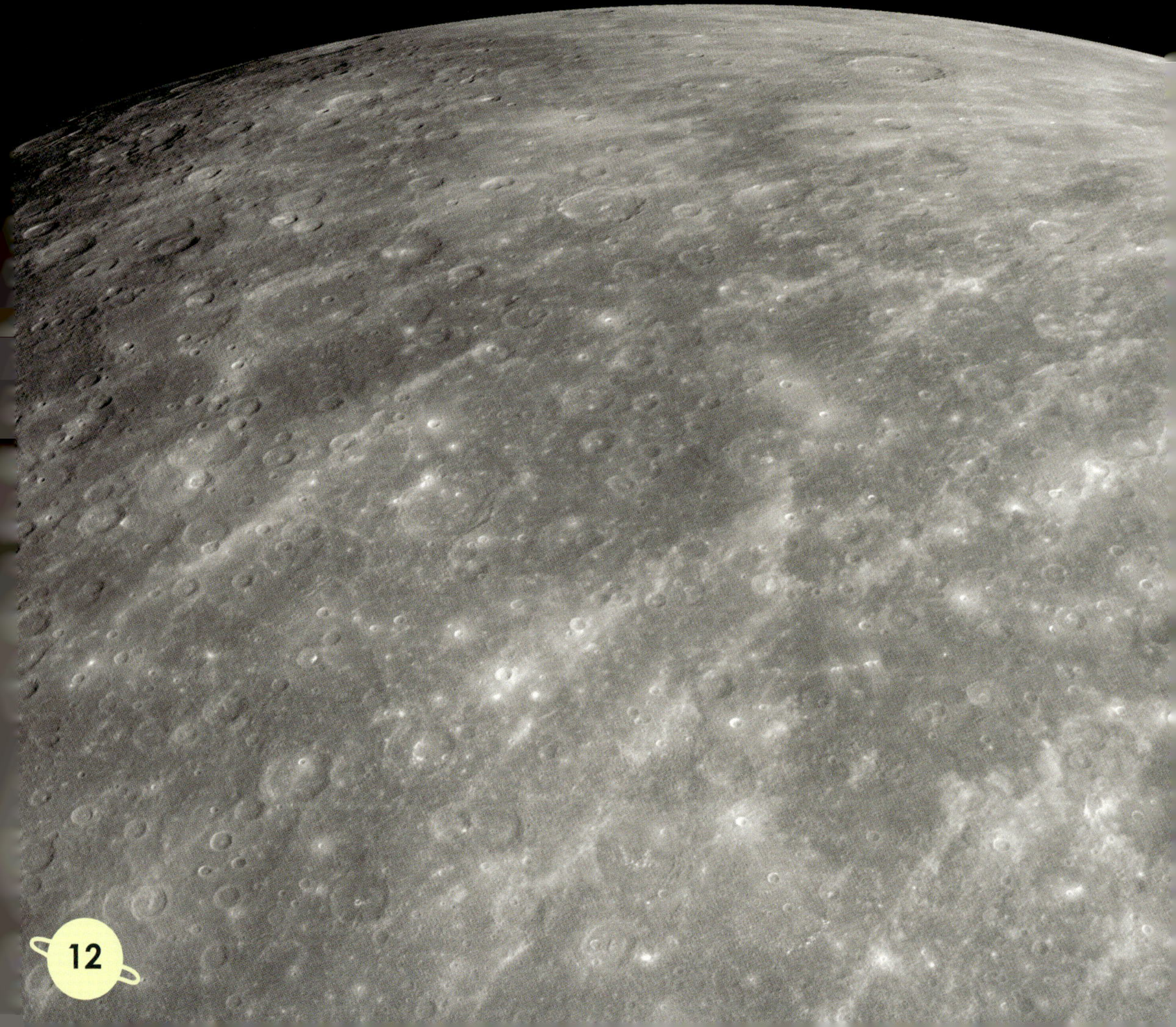

Messenger is one of the spacecraft that has been to Mercury. It found that there is ice in deep **craters** at Mercury's north **pole**! This ice never melts because sunlight doesn't reach it.

Messenger

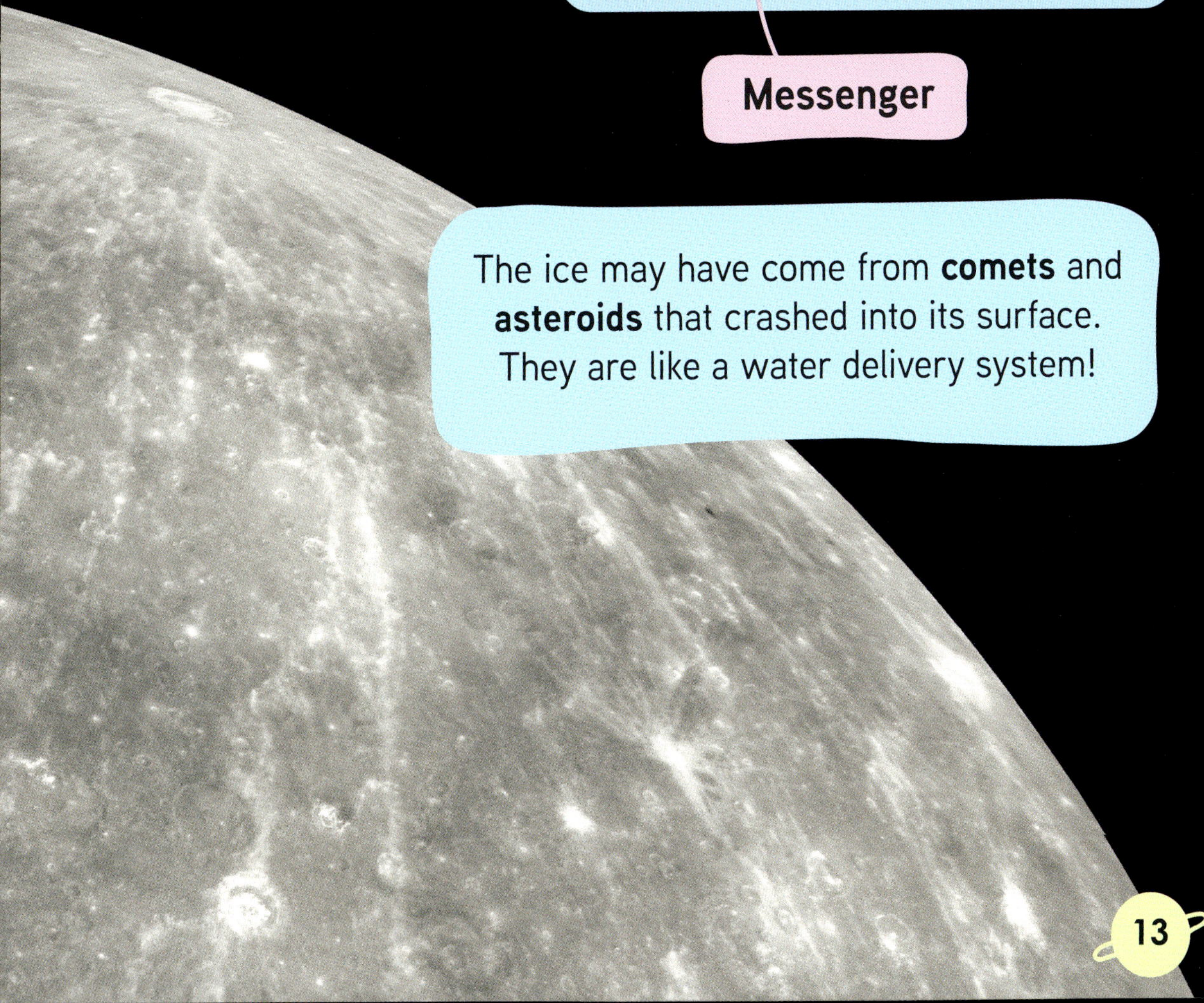

The ice may have come from **comets** and **asteroids** that crashed into its surface. They are like a water delivery system!

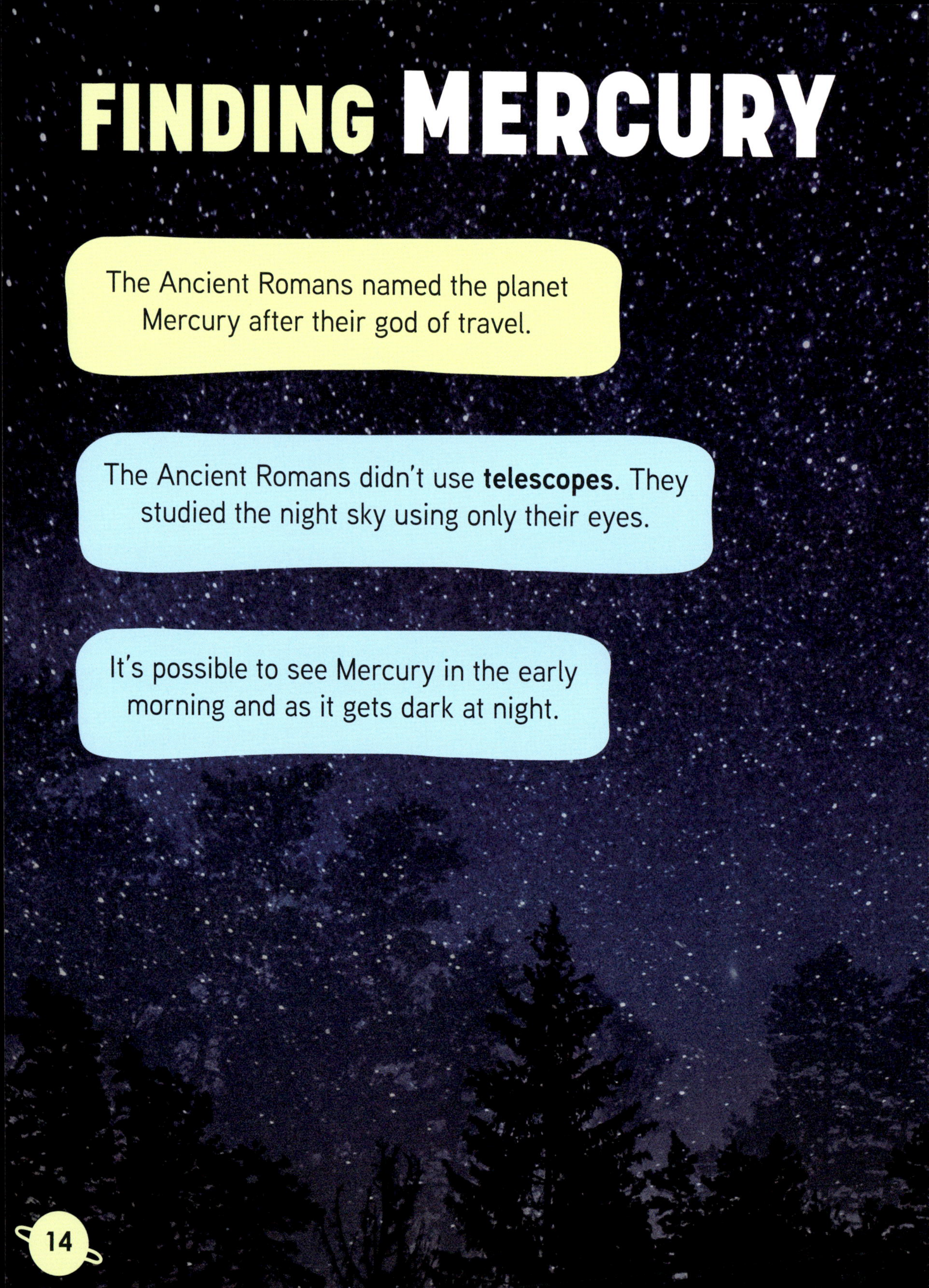

FINDING MERCURY

The Ancient Romans named the planet Mercury after their god of travel.

The Ancient Romans didn't use **telescopes**. They studied the night sky using only their eyes.

It's possible to see Mercury in the early morning and as it gets dark at night.

But it can be tricky. To see Mercury from Earth, we have to look towards the Sun, which is very dangerous! Looking directly at the Sun damages our eyes.

MERCURY'S SURFACE

Mercury is a rocky planet. Its surface looks a lot like the Moon.

It's covered in craters that were created by comets and asteroids crashing into it over billions of years.

The Caloris Basin is the largest crater on the planet. It's 1,550 miles (2,500 kilometers) wide! A giant rock hit Mercury so hard that it made the crater and cracked the surface on the other side!

The camera on **NASA**'s Messenger spacecraft that took this photo made the colors of the planet much brighter than they actually are!

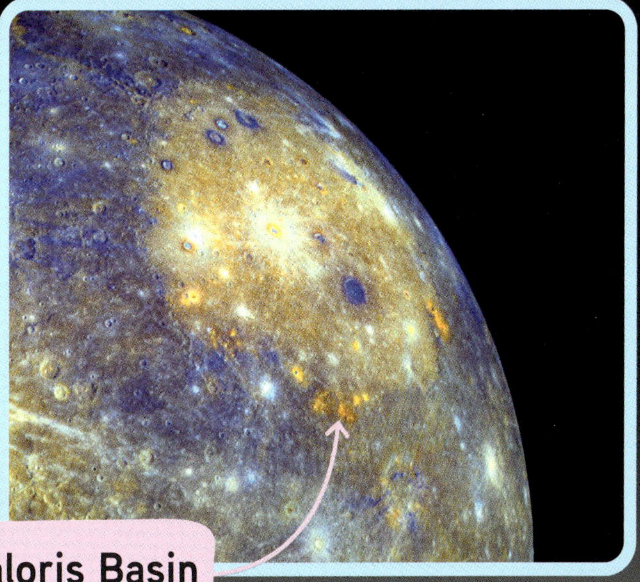

WHY DO WE STUDY PLANETS?

Scientists who study other planets are like space detectives. Their work helps us understand more about our own planet!

They are also looking for valuable materials like rare **minerals** that can be used on Earth for things like energy.

They are also searching to see if there is another planet just like Earth!

FACT FILE

Scientists have several ways that they can study Mercury – but they also have to be careful!

The **Hubble Space Telescope** is forbidden from viewing Mercury because light from the Sun would cause it too much damage.

The Hubble Space Telescope

Scientists used **fissures** in Iceland to learn about Mercury's ice. Ice hidden beneath the surface doesn't melt because sunlight can't reach it!

WHAT'S NEXT?

Most missions to study space are planned by **space agencies** from all over the world. They build rockets and **robots** and sometimes send **astronauts** into space!

Japan Aerospace and the **European Space Agency** launched a joint mission to Mercury in 2018. BepiColombo has completed multiple **flybys**, collecting data and photographs for scientists.

BepiColombo's mission is to take a closer look and learn more about Mercury's surface!

BepiColombo's rocket

GLOSSARY

Asteroids – small space rocks that orbit the Sun.

Astronauts – people trained to travel into outer space.

Atmosphere – the gases that surround a planet.

Comets – objects made of dust and ice that orbit the Sun.

Core – the middle of a planet.

Craters – large holes that have been created by something hitting the ground.

Earth day – the amount of time that a day lasts for on Earth (24 hours).

European Space Agency – an agency run by a group of countries in Europe that studies outer space.

Fissures – a split or crack in the ground.

Flybys – the closest approaches of a spacecraft to a planet or moon.

Hubble Space Telescope – a telescope in orbit around Earth.

Japan Aerospace Exploration Agency – an agency in Japan that studies outer space.

Minerals – substances that are found in things like rocks, sand, and soil.

NASA – the National Aeronautics and Space Administration is an agency that deals with space exploration.

Orbit – the path taken by one object circling around another object in space.

Pole – the point furthest north or south on a planet.

Robots - machines controlled by a computer that can do tasks on their own without a human.

Solar radiation – a type of energy created by the Sun.

Solar system – the Sun and everything that moves around it.

Space agencies – organizations that design and launch missions to explore space.

Telescopes – instruments that make faraway objects appear bigger.

Picture credits:
(t=top; b=bottom; m=middle; l=left; r=right):

NASA: images-assets.nasa.gov/image/PIA10359/PIA10359~orig.jpg 17tr; images-assets.nasa.gov/image/PIA16549/PIA16549~orig.jpg 8-9bg; images-assets.nasa.gov/image/PIA13508/PIA13508~orig.jpg 12-13bg. Unknown 9tl. Shutterstock: 3D Sculptor 13tr; Alexandra Lande 23tl; Alones 22-23bg; Artsiom P 20bl; Buradaki 6-7bg, 10-11bg; Davido Caridl 2-3bg; Istiana wati 14-15bg; Iva Foto 4-5bg; Jurik Peter 16-17bg; Max Dallocca 8br; Muratart 15mr; NASA Images 1bg, 8br, 20-21bg; Procy 24bg; Shivam Chy 18-19bg; T.Schneider 21mr; Waniga Ashan 2-3bg.

Every effort has been made to trace the copyright holders, and we apologize in advance for any unintentional omissions. We would be pleased to insert the appropriate acknowledgments in any subsequent edition of this publication.